FEARLESS
Entertaining

FEARLESS
Entertaining

JOHN DAVID WILLIAMS
CATHERINE HANSEN STRANGE

PHOTOGRAPHY BY
BRENT WALLACE

FEARLESS ENTERTAINING PRESS, LLC
HATTIESBURG, MISSISSIPPI

Without you,
it would have been a lonely walk,
and not nearly as much fun!

To our families and friends
who make everything
possible.

INFORMATION

IT BEGINS WITH YOU

START SMALL

MAKE IT
COMFORTABLE

HOW MANY
DID YOU SAY?

NOT AT MY HOUSE!

GIVING THANKS

'TIS THE SEASON

To entertain is to share. Whether you are sharing your home, talents, food or yourself, entertaining is the most wonderful and warmest way to give. Seldom is anything more pleasant than getting together with people you enjoy. Feeling confident hosting one of these gatherings can be more rewarding than you could ever imagine.

Over the years as we have worked with clients and entertained in our own homes, we have been amazed at how others wish to entertain more often, or to entertain at all. However, the obstacles which they feel are keeping them from doing so are numerous. Their concerns range from not having the correct serving pieces, right location, and knowledge of basic etiquette, to the overall fear of failure. Where as a society have we gotten so off-track? When did it become more important to get it right than to get together at all? What is right, anyway? And who said so?

We have found that the fondest memories people enjoy recalling are those of entertaining and being entertained. But when asked to recall the least favorite memories of the past 60 days few could recall any. What does that say about the power of hospitality? Could it be that the warmth of someone's home, the kindness of being extended an invitation, the breaking of bread with new friends, as well as old, can rise far above the memories of boredom, concerns or pain? If so, what would happen if we all committed to entertain more? Think what it might do for our streets and neighborhoods if all decided to get together more often. How might this affect our communities? What a wonderful goal and easy to achieve - but first we must get past the fear of entertaining and concern for those things that just do not matter.

It all begins with this book. There is nothing good about fear and it can easily be conquered by the growing joy, confidence and enthusiasm these pages will give you. Step-by-step, you will learn how to first take time for yourself, and then, with a relaxed attitude, apply your own personality and style to your own events.

Get Ready to Fearlessly Entertain!

How We Hope You Will Use This Book

After searching for a well-rounded entertaining book at the request of clients and friends, we found that there was little available that was not comprised of 80 percent cookbook and very little on the overall inspiration and planning of the total event. We then researched the availability of older books, where we found some great ones mainly from the mid-1960s. Even though they were better balanced in their information, they were not applicable for the busy lives most of us live today. So we have written this book on the most frequent requests, the most asked questions and the greatest fears regarding entertaining. The concept is simple. Take a deep breath, slow down for just a moment, and then begin small. Once you are confident and relaxed enough to enjoy your own party you have achieved what most agree is the number one characteristic of a successful host.

We hope that you will allow this book to inspire you, expand your ideas and then implement them. You will begin with the inspiration and invitation for each event and then view the overall setting just as your guests would. This book will stress the fact that nothing ever goes as planned and how some of our biggest disasters have turned into our most memorable successes.

The book begins with the smallest of parties, YOU; then, for you and your closest friend; next on to four, six, eight; and up to events for hundreds. As you grow in comfort with your entertaining skills you will find that you also grow more comfortable with larger groups and more elaborate plans. More than anything, our hope is that this book is one you, your family and your friends will use for many years.

Fearless -
It Begins with You !

LIFE IS CONSTANTLY PULLING US FROM EVERY DIRECTION. IT IS HOW WE COPE WITH THE PULLING THAT MAKES THE DIFFERENCE.

WHEN ENTERTAINING, IT ALL BEGINS WITH YOU. HOW YOU ARE FEELING AT THE TIME OF AN EVENT SETS THE TONE FOR ANY CELEBRATION, LARGE OR SMALL. A CALM, POSITIVE HOST IS ASSURANCE FOR A SUCCESSFUL GATHERING.

TAKING TIME FOR YOURSELF IS A NECESSITY TO REFRESH AND REBUILD. THIS CAN MAKE A DIFFERENCE IN HOW WE ARE ABLE TO ENJOY EVERY ASPECT OF OUR DAILY LIVES, AS WELL AS BEING PREPARED FOR THE UNEXPECTED.

Hospitality Begins Within

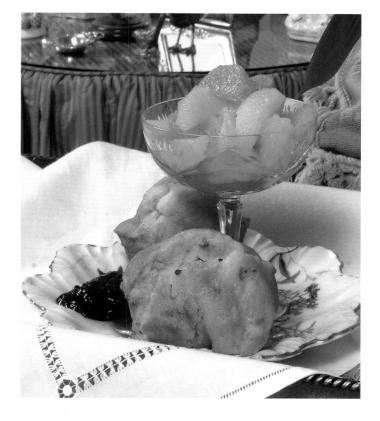

Treat Yourself

Reaching Out

1 Hospitality Begins Within

Being successful does not necessarily require a lot of hard work but always calls for a well thought-out plan and the decision to implement it. This can seldom be accomplished in the midst of chaos. Find a quiet place where you can be alone and begin to reflect and dream.

Take time for yourself regularly, and you will begin to see how the quality of everything you do improves.

Our friend Susan, as busy as she is between business, family and fund raising, claims that her productivity would be greatly diminished if she did not make sure that she spent at least one morning every so often caring for herself. Susan accomplishes this by turning off her phones, locking herself in her bedroom or bath and asking her family that she not be disturbed.

2 Treat Yourself

We all know that life consists of much more than a long bath or breakfast in bed, but taking time for yourself is what is needed to become an exceptional host. As a host your most important role is to make sure your guests feel welcomed and comfortable. The only way this can be accomplished is to first feel relaxed and at ease yourself.

*Whether royalty
or a working mother,
setting aside time to
treat yourself is essential.
Breakfast in bed is a
great place to start.*

*Indulge yourself with little things that
bring you joy. Placing these blue birds
on your breakfast tray could be just the
gesture that brightens your day.*

Surround yourself with the foods, music and the things that you love. You would not cut corners when preparing an environment or meal for your guests; practice the same courtesies and attentions for yourself. After taking the time and effort for yourself on a regular basis, you will become prepared to extend your hospitality to others.

3 ~ Reaching Out

As hectic as our world is today the mere thought of taking time for yourself is difficult, but achievable and habit-forming once you've experienced its satisfaction and joy. The next step to being a gracious host is reaching out to those around you. Entertaining most often begins with an invitation. However, hospitality can be extended from home with the simple, yet effective, power of the pen.

Mary Virginia, a good friend to so many in the community, begins each day with a cup of coffee and her pen. Every morning she takes the time to correspond. Most often her correspondence is with those who are dealing with the loss of a loved one, facing an illness, or just needing an uplifting note. Those who are on the receiving end of Mary Virginia's daily notes attest to their "healing" power. For many, this is one of the few opportunities they have to connect with a caring friend.

Flowers do not have to be arranged, food does not have to be prepared, and your house does not have to be cleaned to touch others' lives through the power of the pen.

Start Small

As with any new endeavor, you must first crawl before you walk. This certainly applies to entertaining as well. Whether wanting to learn how to host your own events or a seasoned hostess desiring to perfect and redefine your entertaining style, start small and surround yourself with friends who are forgiving and fun.

Garden Tea for Two

Luncheon "Four" Friends

Elegant Dinner for Six

4 ~ A Garden Tea for Two

A handwritten invitation dropped off at the door adds a personal touch.

The fern motif used throughout this event came from a live fern leaf that was computer-scanned, color-altered, and re-sized for each different use.

Mary Jefferies Kerry

Reg:
The weather is
beautiful and everything
is in bloom — let's
have tea in the
garden tomorrow
at 4:00 — my quaint
house. — Mary

1117 Porcelain Berry Road
Dahlonega, Georgia

Inviting your best friend or next-door neighbor over for afternoon tea can be very easy. Play with a color scheme or theme that will be the inspiration used as the common thread throughout your occasion. Choose a small corner anywhere! The garden is the launching pad for this tea for two.

Making the event more complicated than needed will discourage you from entertaining. Try using what you have first. Get creative by pulling what you already own from other parts of your garden or home to make an impact.

The garden inspiration for this tea makes it easy to play off the ferns and beautiful plants.

The grapevine wreath is enhanced with living plants and embellished with a few cut flowers placed in water picks.

Whether using custom linens or vintage family cloths, pulling items together within the same color scheme creates a wonderful visual effect.

A teacart pulled close to the table allows for easy access and a beautiful backdrop

Experimenting with menus, etiquette, and levels of formality with those closest to you will allow you to become more confident as a host and whet your palette to continue trying new things.

Something as simple as adding a beautiful garnish not only gives a polished presentation but also helps define you as a host who has an eye for detail.

Using lemon drops in place of sugar cubes or including edible flowers within the food and beverage are both unexpected and fun!

The garden theme, along with the colors green and white, are the common threads that run throughout the china and linens.

Menu

Fresh Strawberries
in a
Cinnamon-Amaretto
Cream Sauce

Cucumber and Dill
Sandwiches

Open-Faced Mini Tomato
Sandwiches

Apricot-Ginger Scones
with
Pink Champagne Jelly

A jar of pink champagne jelly topped with a live fern leaf accompanied a plate of apricot-ginger scones, sending the guest home with a taste of the afternoon.

5 Lunch "Four" Friends

*A*s your comfort with entertaining grows, so should your guest list. Plan a lunch including four well-acquainted friends. This will keep the conversation and laughter flowing. A relaxed occasion such as this allows you to enjoy your own get-together while broadening your entertaining style.

The host's love for this china pattern was the inspiration for the lighthearted luncheon.

Once again, repetition of the same two colors throughout the setting allows for the use of mixed patterns. This presents a fresh, cheerful feeling.

Clustering individual moss-covered gerber daisies creates a hassle-free centerpiece for this poolside luncheon.

A bowl of lemons on each plate is an unexpected touch that informs the guests of the luncheon theme and is easily removed in order to serve the meal.

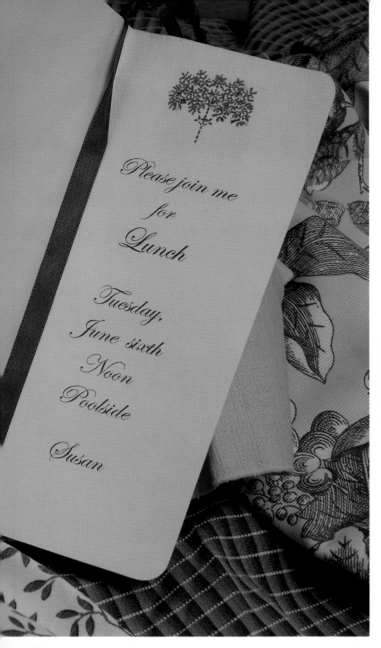

Please join me
for
Lunch

Tuesday,
June sixth
Noon
Poolside

Susan

Do not underestimate the powerful impact paper can have on carrying out the theme of your table. Get creative, or allow your stationer to help. Many stationery shops now offer custom design work. The possibilities are endless!

Jillian

A stenciled lemon tree was used to carry out the lemon theme on the inside of the invitations.

A coordinating blue and yellow toile fabric was computer-scanned to create the outside of the invitation.

An individual gerber daisy plant purchased at a garden center creates an interesting place card holder/parting gift. The daisy container was covered with sheet moss using adhesive spray.

Lemons were used throughout the table creating an inexpensive but fresh table accessory.

A simple slice in a lemon makes a perfect place card holder.

After investing too much time searching for the perfect lemon tree we decided to make our own by wiring lemons to an existing rubber tree. Living plants tucked at the base along with additional lemons completed the look. Using living plants as a centerpiece offers the host a decorating accessory as well as a keepsake after the event.

Menu

Spring Green Salad
with
Candied Fruit
and
Lemon-Raspberry
Dressing

Lemon-Vegetable Pasta

Pucker-up Lemon Squares

6-

Elegant Dinner for Six

More formal settings and menus will become easier as you learn to think outside the box. Serving dinner in front of the living room fireplace, using sofas for seating, creates a warm, relaxed and less intimidating atmosphere.

Using flowers that indicate the last of winter and the first sign of spring are reason alone to celebrate. The English dogwood and camellias used here can be found in many gardens in the South. Use what is accessible to you, then drape and tuck them everywhere. One thing is for sure- you can't beat the price!

When planning a more formal meal think about hiring assistance for the evening. Whether to prepare, serve, or just clean up, consider bringing in the troops.

Many of the finest restaurants are now offering pickup, which can then be brought home, placed on your china, garnished and served. If you feel this removes you too far from your event, another option is to give your recipes to a caterer to prepare for you. Most are more than happy to do this. We do suggest you ask someone to serve during your seated events. We have missed many of our own parties by trying to do it all.

57

Menu

Pan Seared Tuna
with
Stuffed Jalapenos and Avocado Cream

Pan Roasted Pork Chop
with
Peach Barbecue Sauce

Caramelized Onion and Cheddar Cheese Grits

Bittersweet Chocolate and Praline Tart

Make It Comfortable

Choosing a familiar and loved location to entertain, such as a favorite spot to picnic, a cozy wine cellar or a seated dinner at the family lake house often dictates comfort and relaxation for all. These locations may also help you set your theme with the surroundings serving as your decorations. Add simple or favorite foods and, once again, your event is an enjoyable success. Comfortable setting, comfortable friends, and comfortable food create the perfect combination for a wonderful time for guests and host.

7

Impromptu Picnic

8

"Cellar"bration

9

Dinner at the Lake House

7 Impromptu Picnic

*I*mpromptu is the key word. Spur-of-the-moment entertaining usually succeeds because it's unexpected. The best and only invitation needed for one of these events is the phone or "hollering" over your neighbor's fence. These forms of invitations are fine especially when the mood is casual and the point is getting together.

A quick visit to your local deli and produce stand is all that is needed for this event. Pull out your quilts or picnic cloths along with your basket, and the decor is set. In every case this celebration is casual. Do not hesitate to accept the offer of a guest bringing an item for an impromptu event. Very often it allows them to feel included and welcomed.

If time permits add a special or unexpected touch such as a batch of your family's favorite cookies.

A frozen ice sleeve around your wine bottle is a unique way to keep your beverage cool without using an ice bucket or cooler.

Dress up any clear punch by using frozen green grapes in addition to ice.

Menu
Assorted Meats, Cheeses, Breads and Fruits
Henington House Choco Choco Chocolate Chip Cookies
Crisp Cool Pinot Grigio
Iced White Grape Juice and Ginger Ale Punch

8 "Cellar" bration

We realize that not everyone has a wine cellar. However, identifying a unique location to entertain takes the hassle out of planning an event. With little effort, a gathering can be pulled together using the location's decor and supplies created around the family initial.

The family initial on the entrance gate gave inspiration to invitations and parting gifts.

PLEASE JOIN ME
FOR A
CELEBRATION OF WINES
THURSDAY EVENING
SEPTEMBER FIFTEENTH
SEVEN O'CLOCK

THE WINE CELLAR
OF
FIVE MAPLE ROAD

DAVID LEE

FROM THE
WINE CELLAR
OF
DAVID LEE

Stylish, unique paper plates are appropriate for gatherings that are casual and frequent.

Keep in mind that not everyone drinks alcoholic beverages. Offering soft drinks, juices and bottled water is the sign of a thoughtful host.

The growing interest in the diversity of beer encouraged this host to display a selection in an iced-down bucket. The colorful labels, as well as their unique origins, draw attention and conversation even for those who do not partake.

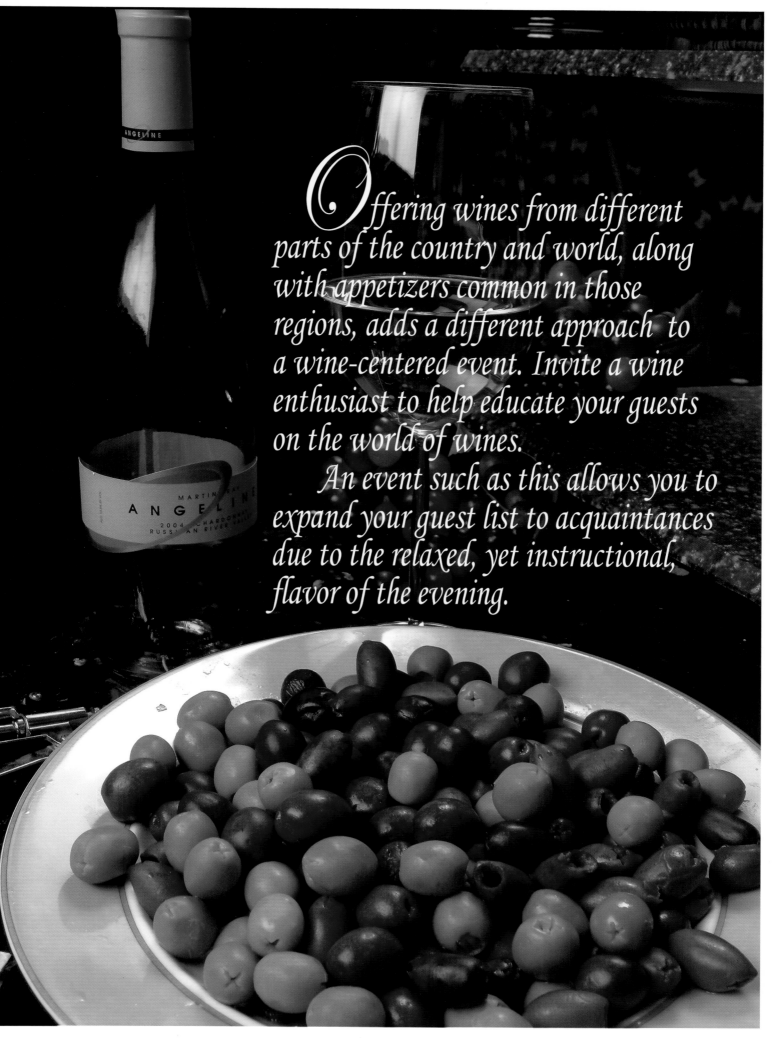

Offering wines from different parts of the country and world, along with appetizers common in those regions, adds a different approach to a wine-centered event. Invite a wine enthusiast to help educate your guests on the world of wines.

An event such as this allows you to expand your guest list to acquaintances due to the relaxed, yet instructional, flavor of the evening.

Menu

Assorted Crackers, Cheeses, Olives and Grapes

Port and Gorgonzola Cheese Spread

Vegetable Confetti Squares

It's a Party! Marinated Shrimp

Cheddar Bacon Dip

9 ~ Dinner at the Lake House

Because of the location the afternoon is a success long before the first guest hits the kitchen screen door. Gathering at this lake house has been a tradition for two families and three generations. Memories, stories and the generous hospitality of its owners keep alive the enchantment of this much-loved location.

Dinner at the Lake House

9/9/99

Dinner at the Lake House
to celebrate the
Last Lazy Days of Summer

Sunday afternoon, August 25
#5 Reel Fish Road

The Halliwells

*Bring your favorite fish tale

Go Fish!

Did someone say, "fish"? Yes, fish, fish, fish! With the location dictating a theme as obvious as this, you are halfway there. Whether you have collected for years or recently hit the local thrift stores, repetition of a theme can make it fun, easy, and will assure you to look like a professional!

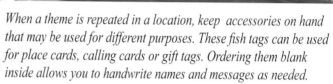

When a theme is repeated in a location, keep accessories on hand that may be used for different purposes. These fish tags can be used for place cards, calling cards or gift tags. Ordering them blank inside allows you to handwrite names and messages as needed.

Menu

Marinated Tomatoes with Shrimp

Mussel and Pepper Pasta

Artichokes stuffed with
Oyster and Artichoke Heart Stuffing

Trout Amandine

Berry Cherry Cobbler

A soup tureen for cobbler? Depression glass mugs for wine? Yes! Now find your favorite rocker and enter the evening relaxing and listening to the lake house fish tales.

Zeus XLVI and Consort Suzanna
accept with pleasure
the kind invitation
of
Her Majesty the Queen
on Saturday, the fifth of February
Two Thousand Five
Under the Big T...
Lake Term...

...nd Duchesses of the Court
...ordially invite you
to a
Dinner Dance
on
...Saturday, February ninth
...nteen hundred and ninety-one
at
seven o'clock in the evening

...Barbara San G...
accepts with...
the kind invitation...
...r Majesty For...
Saturday, the fif...
...r Queen
Two...

How Many Did
You Say?

NOW YOU ARE READY FOR LARGE NUMBERS. DON'T LET THIS INTIMIDATE YOU. IT IS STILL ABOUT BEING AT EASE, SURROUNDING YOURSELF WITH FRIENDS, AND CHOOSING A COMFORTABLE LOCATION. JUST ADD A FEW MORE PEOPLE. THE EVENING IS STILL BUILT AROUND A THEME: FROM SOUP AND SALAD, TO FOOD FROM THE ORIENT, TO A MARDI GRAS COCKTAIL PARTY. BY CREATING DIFFERENT STATIONS THROUGHOUT YOUR HOME THE FOOD IS SELF-SERVED, FUN, INTERESTING AND FITS THE ATMOSPHERE OF THE EVENT. ONCE YOU HAVE ENTERTAINED IN THIS FASHION, THE STYLE WILL FAST BECOME A FAVORITE OF YOURS AS WELL AS YOUR GUESTS.

Soup and Salad

Simply Sushi

Carnival Cocktails

Please join us for

Carnival Cocktails

Friday, the tenth day of February

six of the clock in the evening

preceding the coronation

fifty Kingston Road

The Heidelberg home

Michelle and Web

10 ~ Soup and Salad

Three different soups, three different salads, three different breads and three different stations… This is a perfect party when you want to include everyone.

However, be warned. This event is simple and always such a success that you may never want to entertain any other way!

Station 1 - Dining Room Table
Corn and Crab Bisque
Crunchy Spinach Salad
Three Cheese Bread

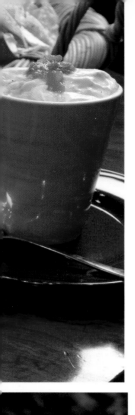

Station 2 - Breakfast Table
Fiesta Stew
Guacamole Salad
Olive and Sun-Dried Tomato Bread

One of the positives of this style of entertaining
is the fact that each location can have a different feel.
Using another set of your dishes, linens and flatware
is acceptable and interesting.

Using Crockpots at each station assures the soup stays warm. Transferring the liner to a more decorative container, such as a copper pot, is another option.

Station 3 - Kitchen Island

New England Clam Chowder
Caesar Salad
Assorted Breads

11 ~ Simply Sushi

This event is simple and specific. Asian-styled parties are very sparse and elegant, little is needed for impact. Select a favorite decorative item for the center of your buffet table and surround it with oversized foliage and orchids. A call to your favorite sushi or oriental restaurant can further simplify the process, especially when preparing for a large crowd. This leaves the food in their hands, saving you time and effort when this type food is not your expertise. We love take-out!

Simply Sushi
is how we are celebrating
Richard Lindsay's
Fortieth Birthday

Please join us
Saturday, January twentieth
Seven o'clock in the evening
333 Honokaa Road
Kona, Hawaii

Mary Jo & Randall Gregory
Lena & Michael James
Jan & Mike Leonard
Minnette Mueller
Lauri & Bob Reed

How simple is this? This tablescape consists of glass platters atop clear glass vases, stacked cake platters, and wineglasses to hold the chopsticks. Assorted sashimi and sushi were placed on the platters at different heights giving this buffet table a multidimensional feel. When entertaining large numbers, the menu does not need to be extensive and can be contained in one location. However, it will need to be replenished throughout the evening.

12 ~ Carnival Cocktails

Please join us for
Carnival Cocktails
Friday, the tenth day of February
six of the clock in the evening
preceding the coronation
fifty Kingston Road
The Heidelberg home

Michelle and Web

Whatever your regional celebrations, cocktails are always an easy way to entertain large numbers. Cocktails often precede other events, which means the food is lighter and the time is limited. Whether Mardi Gras, the symphony or a Broadway play, the theme of the evening is set.

Always provide a spoon when offering nuts or candy in a bowl.

Details such as labeling your bar supplies is important when the bar is self-serve.

Using an adjacent library, the bar setup works well, manned or self-serve. Additional beverage stations may be necessary depending upon your numbers. Another way to avoid congestion is to offer drinks as guests enter the door.

Offering food areas where guests not only can move around,
but also serve and create their own appetizers, encourages interest
and comfort.

Menu
Salmon and Capers

Garlic Cream Spread, Gorgonzola Cheese,
Marinated Sun-Dried Tomatoes, Basil Pesto,
Olive Cream Cheese and Olive Relish

New Orleans-Style Mini Muffulettas

Spinach Rolls and Shrimp Rolls,

Pate, Olives, Fruits and Cheeses

Please join us for

Carnival Cocktails

Friday, the tenth day of February
six of the clock in the evening
preceding the coronation
Fifty Kingston Road
The Heidelberg home

Michelle and Web

Another way to entertain around a particular event, and common in many parts of the country, is a late-night dinner. If this is more than you choose to take on, try inviting everyone back to your home for dessert and coffee.

In the case of a Mardi Gras celebration an over-the-top decorated table is not only appropriate but expected.

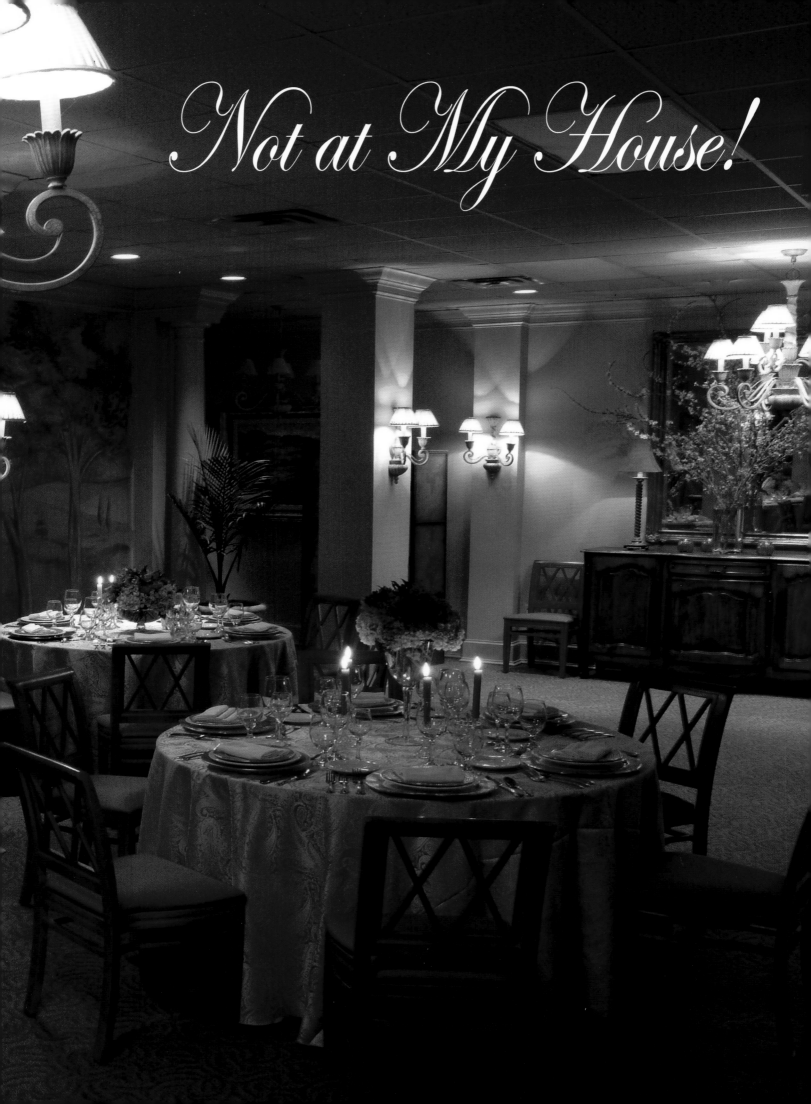

Not at My House!

At times the response "Not at my house" is necessary. Your house is being remodeled, the number of guests are too large for your home, or mere time restraints would make it difficult to pull it all together. This is no excuse not to entertain! Planning an occasion at another facility can be a host's dream. The decisions on theme, guest list, food and decor still have to be made. But usually you have the facility's staff and specialists to guide you with these plans and help you implement them.

Anniversary Dinner 113~

Feast Fit for a King 114~

Under the Big Top 115~

111

13

Anniversary Dinner

M
Please join us for dinner
as we celebrate the
Wedding Anniversary
of
Mr. and Mrs. Michael Eugene McElroy
on Saturday, the third day of February
at seven o'clock in the evening
The Walnut Room

An adjoining room is perfect for serving beverages the first hour of the evening, allowing your guests to visit while others arrive. Make sure there is ample room to move around.

Almost any event is a celebration! The reasons for the gatherings may vary, but staying in tune with the purpose of the party is key. One way this can be accomplished is to let others handle the details. Holding this anniversary dinner at a restaurant's private dining room allows the hosts to stay focused on their guests and the honorees.

Adding personal touches are still an option at a restaurant. Bringing your own china and mixing it with the facility's china, along with renting specialty linens, gives elegance and warmth and adds your personal style. Printed name and menu cards tucked in a simple, folded napkin is another way to enhance the table's decor.

When renting a location to host a party, if available, select a room that offers decorative touches, as well as choices of seating and linens.

Hydrangea, alstromeria and pincushion protea, randomly tucked in a wide-mouth apothecary jar, make beautiful easy centerpieces.

A different utensil for every course may not be available in most homes or most rented facilities. Have no fear, the same fork placed at a different height gives a similar appearance. The dessert fork or spoon may be placed above the plate.

Menu
Veal Stuffed Mushrooms
with
Port Wine and Garlic Sauce

Walnut Circle Salad
with Raspberry Vinaigrette

Oven Roasted Rack of Lamb
with
Mint Demi-Glace Sauce

Pan Roasted Herb Potatoes
Snow Pea Pods Sauteed in Butter

Classic Creme Brulee

14 ~ Feast Fit for a King

Elegance and opulence were the key words that described this feast. Held at a large convention center, this seated dinner for more than 400 made the guests feel as if they were dining in a European castle. This was due to the help of a large party rental company and lighting specialists.

Personalizing each invitation with the guest's name adds to the formality of the event.

Enormous chandeliers hung from the ceiling were rented for the evening's feast.

Flowers in bright colors cascaded over the head table while centerpieces of red roses and gilded fruit were highlighted by the theatrical lighting. Bronze and gold fabric used for table cloths and draping helped make this large facility feel warm and intimate.

15 ~ Under the Big Top

There are more than a thousand invited. Holding an event of this size in your home is usually out of the question. In fact, any event of this size, anywhere, would be a circus! Hey, good idea! The circus theme is now set, and the more the merrier. Hot dogs, cotton candy, snow cones, popcorn, and root beer in a bottle, along with other appetizers and beverages, all fit the theme while making it easy to feed this large crowd.

Clowns, jugglers, and bearded women walking on stilts make all in attendance feel like kids again!

Companies specializing in lighting techniques can make all the difference in how your location looks. The key to decorating a large area is to take up visual space. Lighting may be the most effective way to do this.

Making an impact at a large facility can be a challenge. Ask the facility's managers and your caterer what works best in that particular area. Also inquire about what they have on hand for you to use. The assistance might vary from furniture to yards of draping fabric to the capability to hang decorations extremely high. You will be amazed at how much help this can be. Learn what works, fill in where needed, and make the event your own.

Giving Thanks

There is something good and real about Thanksgiving. Think about it. It is a holiday that is centered completely around being blessed. Other than our cooking preparations it is somewhat uncomplicated. Why do people travel the greatest distances to be with family and friends for this celebration? Keep it relaxed and remember the point is being with the people you care most about. Here are two ways to entertain at Thanksgiving, whether large or small.

Small
Thanksgiving Dinner

Thanksgiving
Breakfast

16~ Small Thanksgiving Dinner

How ever small your gathering, enjoying the holidays are still important. Whoever said you need a crowd to celebrate? Entertaining small can sometimes be more special, allowing you to implement all that you have learned from previous experiences without being overwhelmed.

JOHN DAVID WILLIAMS

Please join me for Thanksgiving dinner on Thursday, November 24 at 7:00 p.m. My home — JD

The interiors of this home gives direction to the holiday decorating. A black and brown toile-covered table, a permanent fixture in the library area, is now pulled center stage as the dining room table. A mixture of chairs and china, along with the host's oriental-inspired decorative pieces complete the look. A collection of gourds, pinecones and greenery, tucked into available spaces, were added to the already-decorated mantel. The feeling of Thanksgiving is abundance - in this

Do not feel you need to undecorate to decorate. Your personal items will be enhanced by the addition of the season's decor.

Menu

Cranberry-Mandarin Orange Salad

Rosemary and Orange
Cornish Game Hen

Olive and Caper Stuffing Tower

Asparagus wrapped with Bacon Pastry

Blueberry Bread

Apple Pecan Pie - a la mode

Preparing for small numbers allows you to give the holiday meal a new twist. A Cornish game hen prepared for each guest is an interesting change from the traditional Thanksgiving turkey. If the truth be told, this was the result of one of our biggest entertaining disasters. When no turkeys were to be found during a last-minute shopping trip, the only choice was to get creative. Much to our surprise our guests thought the special and personal addition of the hens was a

17-
Thanksgiving
Breakfast

Longleaf Plantation

Wren's Nest

Once again a
Thankful Gathering
of
Family and Friends

join us for
Thanksgiving Breakfast

9:00 a.m.
Thanksgiving Morning
Longleaf Plantation
Wren's Nest

Carolyn and Warren

casual

If the saying "home is where your heart is" holds true, then home is the best place to be on Thanksgiving day. If your family is like most, the festivities can be many. Whether watching the parades and football games or fulfilling commitments to both sides of the family, breakfast is the place to begin. Set in the kitchen to enjoy morning beverages while people awake and arrive, an easy breakfast meal served buffet-style can simply feed the multitudes.

Menu
Fried Quail
Scrambled Eggs with Bacon
Hash Brown Potatoes with Chives
Pork Sausage
Homemade Butter Biscuits
with Ma haw Jelly
Coffee, Assorted Juices,
Bloody Marys

When serving buffet-style the plates may be stacked at the buffet, or placed at each individual setting. Silverware and glassware may remain at the table making the transition from the buffet table to the dining area more manageable.

Don't be afraid of scale, especially during the holidays. This table arrangement using a large carved antique deer, moved here from another part of the home, is laden with fresh greenery garlands, pinecones and red pears.

One benefit from using the deer as the centerpiece is that the look can carry through the rest of the holiday season.

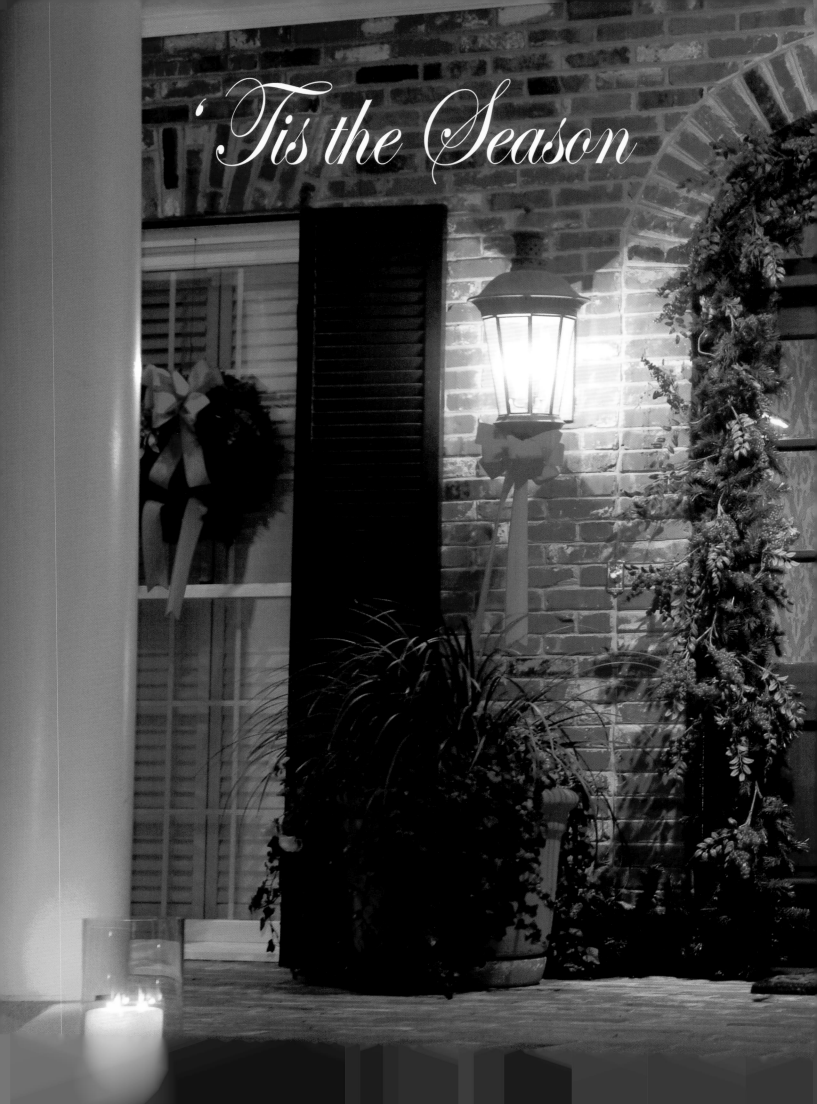

'Tis the Season

WHAT IS YOUR FAVORITE CHRISTMAS MEMORY? THAT STINGRAY BIKE WITH THE BANANA SEAT, DECORATING THE TREE WITH YOUR FAMILY, OR EVERY YEAR GOING TO THE SMITH'S HOUSE AFTER THE CHURCH CHRISTMAS PAGEANT? WHATEVER YOUR MEMORIES, THE HOLIDAYS ARE MAGICAL. THE CELEBRATIONS ARE MANY. FROM CAROLING WITH CHILDREN TO ELEGANT GATHERINGS, THE SECRET IS NOT TO GET OVERWHELMED. START EARLY, BE PREPARED, KEEP YOUR GOALS REALISTIC AND REMEMBER THE REASON WE CELEBRATE THIS WONDERFUL TIME OF YEAR.....

IT'S BEGINNING TO LOOK A LOT LIKE CHRISTMAS!

Sweet Caroling

*Home,
Ready for the Holidays*

18~ Sweet Caroling

Young and old, we are all children at heart. This warm, whimsical celebration after an evening of caroling will make anyone see Christmas through the eyes of a child. Lollipops, jawbreakers, salt-water taffy and vintage-wrapped chocolate bars serve as decorations and are just what is needed to entice this crowd.

A Sweet Celebration!

Please join us for
dessert after caroling
Friday, December 18
8:00 p.m.
208 Oak Lane

The Murpheys

*As visions of sugar plums
danced in their heads...*

Everybody ends up in your kitchen anyway, so why not start there? The island is a perfect stage for this candy wonderland. Using this fun Christmas tree as the centerpiece, then creating levels and layers by tucking in candy jars and the host's Santa collection, makes this an eye-opening presentation. The candy and sweets theme is carried throughout with peppermint plates, cookie mugs and ornaments. Even though the overall feeling is traditional, the colors are not. Lime-green is fast becoming a Christmas basic. Including it in your decor adds to the fun!

Placing ornaments and decorations among your holiday treats adds a bit of whimsy.

Adding peppermints to your hot cocoa, or hot candies to your cider gives a spicy holiday flavor to your beverages.

Gumdrops hot glued to a note holder turns a desk basic into a decoration.

When using your favorite holiday recipes for baked goods and candy there is no question you will be a hit. Or… you can call your local bakery or gourmet shop, pick them up, have extra time on your hands, and still be a hit!

Not everyone can fit in your kitchen during a party this large. Remember, offering food, beverages and entertainment throughout encourages your guests to feel welcomed in other areas of your home. Sending your guests home with a parting gift is another sign of a thoughtful host. Choosing one that represents the evening will ensure an everlasting memory.

Parting gifts placed close to the front door encourages guests to take home a taste of the evening.

Cookies and other baked goods placed in adjacent sitting areas tempt your guests to move freely throughout your home.

Including the front door's decor in your evening's theme can give a much-anticipated hint of what is to come.

A gift for your host, such as a holiday guest towel, or ornament, is always a kind gesture.

19~
Home, Ready for the Holidays

A home ready for the holidays is a magnificent way to give. This cherished time of year often slips by us due to our lack of preparation or tendencies to overload. Step back. Choose one or two areas to decorate on a grand scale, and add small holiday vignettes throughout the rest of your home.

Perhaps this year, don't plan that big party. Instead, be ready to open your doors to friends and neighbors that stop by, and invite them into your home for coffee or tea. This is a gracious form of entertaining, and a wonderful holiday gift to all!

Your dining room table is always a great place to make a large statement. During the holidays use your decorative items that are already in place and decorate around them for a different twist on the traditional. The oriental vase and figurines shown here are a great example of how this can work.

A long, narrow centerpiece would be perfect for hosting a holiday buffet or seated dinner. Add elegance by choosing accents such as ribbons and ornaments that fit the color scheme of the room. Placing assorted glasses filled with fresh cranberries and kumquats among the garland adds to the seasonal spirit.

Wonderful

Weddings

MAKING YOUR DREAMS COME TRUE IS WHAT WEDDING PLANS ARE ALL ABOUT. MOST YOUNG WOMEN HAVE BEEN THINKING ABOUT THIS DAY SINCE AGE FIVE. MAKING IT A REALITY CAN BE EXCITING AND CHALLENGING. THE KEY TO ANY GREAT WEDDING IS MAKING SURE THAT THERE IS A CLEAR REFLECTION OF THE BRIDE AND HER FAMILY. STAY CALM AND ORGANIZED, AND YOU WILL ENJOY YOUR OWN WEDDING.

THROUGH IT ALL IT IS IMPORTANT TO KEEP IT IN PERSPECTIVE. WHETHER YOU ARE MARRIED ON THE BEACH OR IN A CATHEDRAL, WHETHER YOUR FLOWERS ARE ORCHIDS OR SUNFLOWERS, THE RESULTS ARE THE SAME.

YOU ARE STILL MARRIED!

20~ Bridal Brunch

24~ Wedding at Home

22~ In a Place of Worship

marriage, it is an ever fixed mark   *Shakespeare*

A Bridal Brunch

Please join us for a
Bridal Brunch
Celebrating the Ar...
honoring
Kathleen Kelleh...
and her
Bridesmaids

Thirty-One Flower Meadow Road
N... ...a, Louisiana 59401

The favor of
a reply
is requested by
March twenty fifth
Beverly
504-310-2202

Friday, the fifth of ...
eleven in the morni...
...irty-one Flower Mead...
the home of
Susan Rutlan...

marriage, it is an ever fixed mark
Shakespeare

A Bridal Brunch

*I*t can be helpful to follow a central theme even when planning a party as traditional as a bridal brunch. A love for the arts by both the bride and the host influenced this event's theme. Using one of the host's miniature oil paintings as the inspiration for the invitation made clear the atmosphere for the brunch.

Greet your guests with an assortment of muffins and refreshing morning beverages.

Menu
Orange-Cranberry Muffins
Fresh Orange Juice
Mimosas

Often the bridal brunch or luncheon is the first event of the wedding festivities. As in the case of most events, it is important to offer refreshments while your guests gather. This time also provides the opportunity for those who do not know each other to get acquainted.

When hosting an event with numbers larger than your dining room table will seat, use other parts of your home to accommodate your guests. A partner-style writing desk with pull-out leaves serves as an interesting table for six in the library.

Seating your guests in various locations allows you to create different looks and feelings with china, flowers, and collections in each room. This is also beneficial in setting the table since few own enough of one pattern to serve this many guests. Renting or borrowing is also an option when needing to expand your dishware, silverware and glassware.

With larger numbers and gatherings, where not everyone is acquainted, providing place cards is important. Giving some thought to the seating assignment at each table will assure that every guest is comfortable.

Adorned bridesmaids' gifts can be used as place cards and table decorations. Personalized stationery is always a beautiful gift.

Menu
Duck Salad with
Apple Cinnamon Currant Sauce
Crab cakes with Remoulade Sauce
Strawberry Custard French Toast

Color-coordinating the table accessories such as the place cards and menu cards enhances the look of any table. An individual vase of roses accentuates each place setting.

The dining room is the second setting for this bridal brunch. Using family china and silver always adds to a well-appointed table.

The most casual setting is found in the host's breakfast room which adjoins the kitchen. In times past this might have been frowned upon. Not now! Being placed in the most comfortable area of the home is a reflection of how close the host feels to you. If you choose to use an area such as this consider having it catered. This will allow the kitchen to stay relatively neat and provide freedom for the host to move from room to room.

We love to mix patterns! China, silver and crystal can be mixed to add a more personal touch to each place setting. Taking the lead from the casual setting, each guest's flower arrangement was presented in a teacup .

21-
Wedding at Home

If a wedding is to be a reflection of the bride and her family, then holding the ceremony and reception at home is most certainly the best way to accomplish this. At home, the feeling and decor is already set, and enhancing its beauty is all that is needed.

Every location has its limitations. In this case, the guest list to the wedding ceremony was kept to family and the closest of friends. The ceremony was held underneath a large tent. Rented guest chairs were moved after the wedding to accommodate the seating inside the home and open up the dance floor for the reception. Wedding guests enjoyed passed hors d'oeuvres and champagne while awaiting the arrival of the 300 reception guests. As the guests approached, a violin quartet on the front lawn welcomed them to the reception. Guests enjoyed a cocktail buffet and a night of dancing to celebrate the couple's nuptials.

Due to Hurricane Katrina, which occurred one month prior to the wedding, the couple chose to honor their guests by making a donation to the "Rebuild the Coast Fund" in lieu of parting favors.

The bride's cake, along with guest seating, was featured in the grand family room where the furniture had been removed to create space for the occasion. Small vases of white roses and candles in hurricane globes adorned the tables.

A grand buffet of selected seafood was presented in the family dining room. Other food stations were found throughout the home, as well as outdoors where pasta and crepes were made to order. Two large bars were outdoors to service the guests.

Menu

Smoked Gulf Coast Crab Dip
Smoked Norwegian Salmon Display
Boiled and Chilled Gulf Coast Shrimp
Seared Yellow Fin Tuna
Gingered Wonton Crackers
Spicy Crawfish Tarts

The warmth of the family's breakfast room warranted the bountiful array of fruits, breads and cheeses. Presented in a French-country style, this created a unique and welcoming feel to the additional food station.

Menu

Grilled Vegetables
Assorted Olives
Marinated Artichokes
Fruits
Artisan Breads
Domestic and Imported Cheeses

22 ~ In a Place of Worship

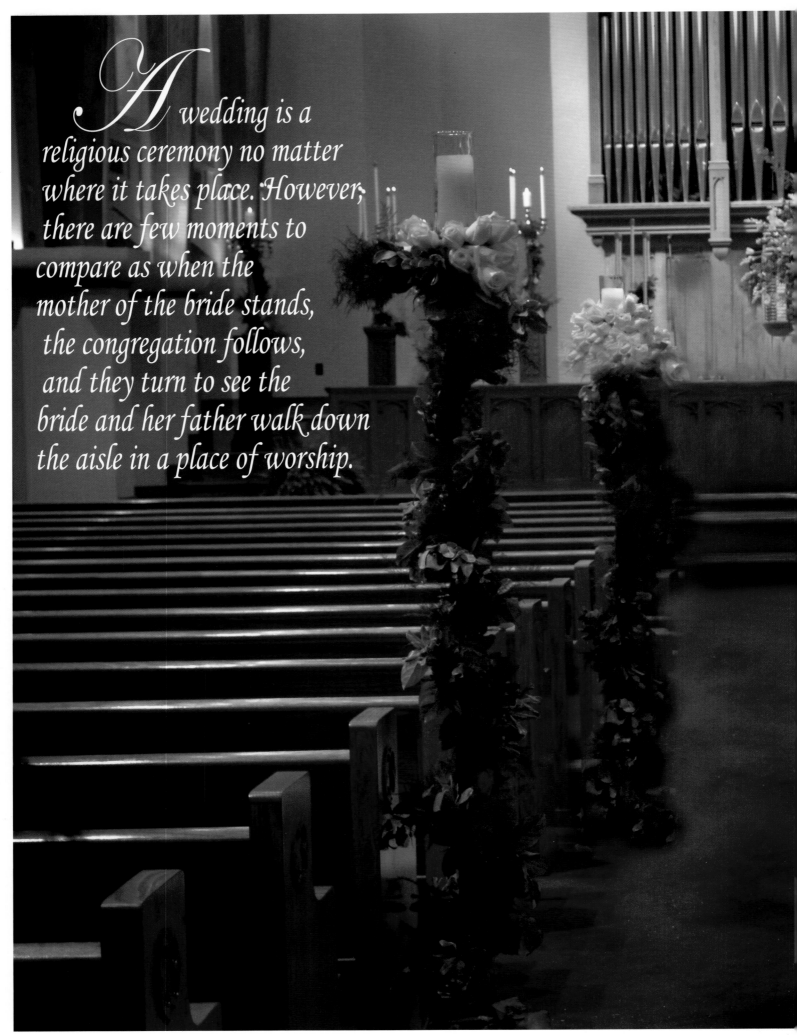

A wedding is a religious ceremony no matter where it takes place. However, there are few moments to compare as when the mother of the bride stands, the congregation follows, and they turn to see the bride and her father walk down the aisle in a place of worship.

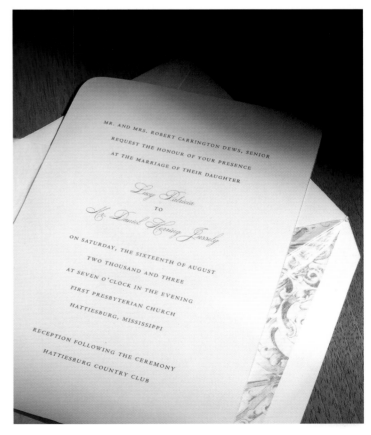

MR. AND MRS. ROBERT CARRINGTON DEWS, SENIOR

REQUEST THE HONOUR OF YOUR PRESENCE

AT THE MARRIAGE OF THEIR DAUGHTER

Lucy Patricia

TO

Mr. Daniel Herring Tweedy

ON SATURDAY, THE SIXTEENTH OF AUGUST

TWO THOUSAND AND THREE

AT SEVEN O'CLOCK IN THE EVENING

FIRST PRESBYTERIAN CHURCH

HATTIESBURG, MISSISSIPPI

RECEPTION FOLLOWING THE CEREMONY

HATTIESBURG COUNTRY CLUB

When beginning wedding preparations, keep in mind that these memories and pictures will be around forever. Consider making selections that are not too trendy. Subtle statements that project style can be accomplished in many different areas. An example are these classic invitations engraved in chocolate-brown, a color also used in the wedding.

Do not assume that the church, country club, photographer, caterer and florist will be available. Secure these bookings as soon as there is a wedding date. If using a wedding planner, make that your first call. The planner can assist you in all wedding details. This will save you time and energy in an already busy period in your life.

Mr. and Mrs. Gary Duncan Wood
request the honour of your presence
at the marriage of their daughter

Jennifer Camille
to
Mr. Howard Bernard Nelson III

Saturday, the seventeenth of June
Two thousand six
six o'clock in the evening
South Highland Presbyterian Church
Birmingham, Alabama

Reception
immediately following the ceremony
The Country Club of Birmingham
Birmingham, Alabama

Mrs. Gu.
802 Moss Cr.
Duluth, Georgia

333 Bedford Road
Hattiesburg, Mississippi 89402

Doctor and Mrs. Douglas Wesley Rouse, junior
request the pleasure of your company
at the marriage of their daughter
Christa Michele
to
John Bancroft Bishop
day, the twenty-second of October
Two thousand and five
o'clock in the evening
Our home
5th Road

The favour of a reply is requested
before the eighth of October

M_____ will _____ attend

Depending on the location of the ceremony the invitation wording will change. In a place of worship the invitation reads "request the honour of your pres-ence." Note that the more formal British spelling of "honour" is used in this instance. If the ceremony is held anywhere else the invitation reads "request the pleasure of your company."

199

The Wedding Celebration
of
Traci Ellen Holmes
and
Douglas Wesley Rouse, III

R

Saturday, the twenty-second of April
two thousand and six
half after six in the evening

First Baptist Church
Hattiesburg, Mississippi

Weddings are about details. From the bride's bouquet to the wording in the program, the details separate one wedding from another. This traditional church wedding reflects the elegant simplicity of the bride's style, while working well with the beauty of the sanctuary. The use of regional greenery and candles in the church's large, stained-glass windows are all that is needed - allowing their beauty to be seen.

After large church weddings, receptions often follow at hotel ballrooms, country clubs, convention centers and other wedding facilities. These locations offer catering services and a helpful staff. Usually a large facility will require more extensive decorating. With this in mind, specialty and theatrical lighting is the best way to stage a large, open area. Consider making this a priority in your wedding budget. Letting the lighting professionals handle your event will add to the elegance of the evening.

It would take many more arrangements to make the visual impact that this one arrangement made with the addition of theatrical lighting.

When choosing a location for your wedding reception it is important to note what the facility offers both architecturally and visually. Often you will find that various settings may require less decorating and offer beautiful grounds to expand the reception.

The above invitation highlighting the Hebrew scripture and the couple's names in copper gives a unique touch to this traditional card. When all guests are not invited to the reception, include a separate reception card. In this case, due to the size of the synagogue, one invitation was engraved for the ceremony and another for the reception.

The traditional Chuppah, lavishly covered in cymbidium orchids, was the centerpiece for this formal wedding.

The bride's cake was featured in the entrance area decorated with live cymbidium orchids, repeating the theme from the Chuppah at the synagogue, while the groom's cake was featured in front of an antique mirror in another area of the club.

Details For Your Wedding

If you are planning a full-scale wedding you will need a minimum of six months to one year to plan the event. Upon your engagement, you need to immediately book the wedding site, reception site, caterer, florist, minister, photographer, videographer, cake designer, musicians for the ceremony and reception, and limousine service.

Arriving at one date when all are available would be difficult, so having time on your side is a plus.

After these time sensitive decisions are made, and before you meet personally with any of these, you must have a budget. Creating one will help define your expectations for this most memorable day. As much as we do not like to talk about money, it will make the process more enjoyable and less stressful if you know your financial parameters.

Regardless of the budget, you can accomplish any style of wedding by controlling the number of guests you invite. Larger numbers generally translate to more invitations, a larger facility, more flowers, more food, and more bars. Weddings in the past 20 years have become larger and less-intimate gatherings. Do not get caught up in the wedding frenzy! Always make sure the wedding is a reflection of the bride and her family's style and sensibilities.

As with any entertaining event it is helpful to have an inspiration, theme and colors to plan your wedding. Usually the bride's favorite color begins the process of choosing her bridesmaids' gowns as well as wedding flowers. Certainly the time of year for the wedding helps in making these decisions.

Two of the most important decisions from which the others will play off of are the wedding gown and the invitation. These more than others set the style and formality of the wedding. Your invitation is the first indication of the direction you have chosen for your wedding. Until recently only white or ivory paper with black engraving was acceptable. Today the most formal invitation companies are offering an array of colors and styles reflecting the trends of the day. Make no mistake - the rules of etiquette and courtesies still apply. If you are wanting to make more trendy selections for your wedding, sometimes they are more appropriate in your pre-wedding celebrations.

Always remember that weddings are about the bride and groom and their commitment to each other. Keeping that in mind will help to alleviate all the unnecessary stress in planning the wedding. As said before, "whether married on a beach or in a cathedral... you are still married."

23 ~
Whew! It's Over!

Whew! The event is over! Everyone had a wonderful time and now it is back to you. That is where you began: dreaming or possibly just curious about entertaining at another level. Now it's time to find a quiet place and make notes regarding the elements you felt made it such a success. Jot down the few things you might have changed or what would have made it easier on you. Relax, reflect on a job well done, and begin planning your next "fearless" event.

Attention to Details

Consort Jane

Using Collections

The Table

Invitations

Recipes

Flowers

Acknowledgments
Locations
Resources

Using Collections

Whether you realize it or not,
you have collected something over the
years. Go to your cabinets, and group
all similar things together. Before
you know it, you will have a collection
of beautiful candlesticks, silver serving
pieces, or the most whimsical childhood
toys. You will find that what you have
collected or held on to over the years
are those things that have meaning, or
bring you joy.

Using these collections can be as simple as grouping them together on a fireplace mantel or a side table in your family room. It is a fact that similar things look better grouped together. Collections offer you decorating inspirations for many of your entertaining events. Take all of your blue and white porcelain, arrange them together on your dining room table, and your centerpiece is done. Add candles and flowers and you have a delightful focal point to receive your guests.

Simply Sushi
is how we are celebrating
Richard Lindsay's
Fortieth Birthday

Please join us
Saturday, January twentieth
Seven o'clock in the evening
333 Honokaa Road
Kona, Hawaii

Mary Jo & Randall Gregory
Lena & Michael James
Jan & Mike Leonard
Minnette Mueller
Lauri & Bob Reed

M
Please join us for dinner
as we celebrate the
Wedding Anniversary
of
Mr. and Mrs. Michael Eugene McElroy
on Saturday, the third day of February
at seven o'clock in the evening
The Walnut Room

We join me for a
Holiday Cocktail Buffet

Wednesday, December 21, 2005

7:30 in the evening

49 Tidewater Road

Julie and Paul Talbot

The favor of a response is requested
601.296.6887

marriage, it is an ever fixed mark
Shakespeare

A Bridal Brunch

Thirty One Flower Meadow Road
Louisiana 59401

The favor of
a reply
is requested by
March twenty fifth
Beverly
504-310-2202

Please join us for a
Bridal Brunch
Celebrating the Arts
honoring
Kathleen Kelleher
and her
Bridesmaids

Friday, the fifth of April
eleven in the morning
Thirty one Flower Meadow Road
the home of
Susan Rutland

MR. AND MRS. ROBERT CARRINGTON DEWS, SENIOR
REQUEST THE HONOUR OF YOUR PRESENCE
AT THE MARRIAGE OF THEIR DAUGHTER

Lucy Patricia

TO

Mr. David Herring Jessely

ON SATURDAY, THE SIXTEENTH OF AUGUST
TWO THOUSAND AND THREE
AT SEVEN O'CLOCK IN THE EVENING
FIRST PRESBYTERIAN CHURCH
HATTIESBURG, MISSISSIPPI

RECEPTION FOLLOWING THE CEREMONY
HATTIESBURG COUNTRY CLUB

Mr. and Mrs. Gary Duncan Wood
request the honour of your presence
at the marriage of their daughter

Jennifer Camille

to

Mr. Howard Bernard Nelson III

Saturday, the seventeenth of June
Two thousand six
six o'clock in the evening
South Highland Presbyterian Church
Birmingham, Alabama

Reception
immediately following the ceremony
The Country Club of Birmingham
Birmingham, Alabama

Invitations

Most appreciate being included, everyone loves being invited. Whether engraved or handwritten, the invitation is the perfect way to reflect the theme and purpose of the celebration. Include all pertinent information: the reason for the gathering; the date, time and location; who is hosting it; the attire; and the appropriate response. The level of formality is easily communicated through the style of the invitation. Leaving no question in the minds of your guests is a sign of a considerate host. With less formal invitations the sky is the limit. Get creative or hire someone who is. Handmade papers, computers, scanners and wonderful stationery shops leave you no excuse not to have the perfect invitation.

Flowers

Flowers are only one element in entertaining, but can set the stage for your occasion like no other. Just as the invitation does, flowers can help define the casualness or formality of any event. Color, scale, and texture in flowers, as well as how they are arranged, are used to let people know they have arrived at a celebration. Camellias out of your yard and arranged in a mint julep cup, gerber daisy plants from your nursery grouped together as your centerpiece, or a huge floral arrangement at a wedding cement the phrase "nothing says it like flowers."

Decide early on if you will bring in a professional to handle the flowers. A small luncheon in your home is certainly different from a reception for hundreds in a ballroom. Hiring a competent florist can help eliminate stress, while making sure that your vision is being carried out.

223

The Table

A table should always be inviting and comfortable no matter what the occasion or level of formality. If your guests are more concerned with which fork to use rather than enjoying the company of those around them, then you, as the host, have missed the mark. Place settings should only include those utensils required for each course. Keep in mind that most people know to use their utensils starting from the outside and working in. Elaborate place settings, though beautiful, can confuse your guests.

Guests will always follow the lead of the host. Being aware of this, a host can make her guests feel at ease from the moment they arrive. At the table, the host gives direction on seating, selecting the first utensil, and the flow of the conversation. Do not be intimidated. Common courtesies such as these will become natural to you as you entertain more.

A Few Favorite Recipes

Entertaining fearlessly includes having recipes, restaurants and caterers you can count on. Here are a few recipes from the different menus. The "Fearless Recipes" are simple and encourage you to incorporate your own twist. The others are straight from the pros - each teaching you a little something unique and varying in complication. Recipes are like entertaining: start simple, become comfortable, and then expand.

Garden Tea for Two
Fearless Recipes
Page 37

Fresh Strawberries in an
Cinnamon-Amaretto Cream Sauce

2 pints fresh strawberries, quartered or whole

Mix together until smooth the following:
8 oz. sour cream
1 C. powdered sugar
1/2 t. ground cinnamon
4 T. amaretto or 1 t. almond flavoring

Pour over strawberries or cluster as shown for dipping.
Garnish and serve cool.
Serves 6.

Cucumber and Dill Sandwiches

2-8 oz. cream cheese (softened)
1 large cucumber, peeled, grated and drained
1/4 C. chopped fresh dill or 1 t. ground dill
1/2 medium onion, grated with juice

Cream ingredients together. Salt to taste.

One loaf of bread with crusts removed.

Spread cucumber mixture on bread.
Cut as desired and serve.

Open-Faced Mini Tomato Sandwiches

Mix together:
2 C. mayonnaise
3/4 C. real bacon bits
1/2 t. meat tenderizer
1/2 C. chopped onions
1/2 C. basil (optional)

1 loaf long slender baguette bread, sliced

Spread mayonnaise mixture on each bread slice. Top with sliced tomato.
Garnish with dab of spread and basil or chopped onions.

Apricot-Ginger Scones

Preheat oven to 400 degrees.

Place in a food processor:
2 1/4 C. all-purpose flour
1/3 C. sugar
1 T. baking powder
2 t. orange peel

Add using off/on button until mixture resembles coarse meal:
11 T. chilled, unsalted butter, cut into small pieces

Transfer mixture to large bowl. Make a well in the center.

Add to well, using fork, stir until just moist:
3/4 C. whipping cream

Mix in:
1/4 C. crystallized ginger
3/4 C. diced apricots

Transfer dough to floured surface and gently knead until smooth, about 8 turns. Divide dough in half; pat each portion into ¾-inch-thick round. Cut into rounds or wedges and transfer to lightly buttered baking sheet, spacing 1 inch apart.

Brush tops with 2 T. whipping cream. Bake scones until light brown, about 18 minutes. If you make them the day before, reheat in 350 degree oven before serving.
Makes 12.

Pink Champagne Jelly

Wash and dry jelly jars, bands and lids. Set aside.

Stir over heat:
2 C. pink champagne
4 C. sugar
Until sugar is completely dissolved.
Remove from heat.

Add:
1 pouch liquid fruit pectin

Mix well and pour immediately into prepared containers, leaving 1/2 inch space at top.
Wipe lip of jar clean and place lids and bands on.
Let stand at room temperature for 24 hours.
Yields 5 cups.

Note: Try substituting white champagne in place of pink and serving it with meats such as duck.

Lunch "Four" Friends
Fearless Recipes
page 43

Spring Green Salad with Candied Fruit and Lemon-Raspberry Dressing

In a bowl mix well:
1 C. raspberry sauce
1/2 C. lemon juice
1/4 C. pineapple-peach preserves

Generously toss
in mixture 1/2 C. each:
Candied mango, sliced
Candied peach, sliced
Candied pineapple chunks
Golden raisins
Whole almonds

With a slotted spoon remove fruit and nuts from mixture, placing on individual plates atop a bed of spring greens.

Thin balance of mixture slightly with more lemon juice if needed and drizzle over the top.
Sprinkle with shredded coconut if desired.
Serves 4-6.

Lemon Vegetable Pasta

Mix well in a large bowl:
1 C. lemon juice
1 C. olive oil
10 garlic cloves, pressed (more or less optional)
2 t. salt
1 t. white pepper.

Place in mixture:
1 large, firm tomato, cut in chunks
1 C. raw broccoli
1/2 C. olives, pitted or sliced
1/2 C. green onions, chopped
Toss well and set aside.

Prepare pasta as directed (any noodle will work).

Drain vegetables from lemon juice mixture.
Toss pasta in balance of mixture thoroughly.
Mix vegetables within pasta or place pasta on a plate and generously pile vegetables on top.
Generously top with grated parmesan cheese or offer it on the side.
Serve hot or cold.

For a heavier meal, add meat such as chicken.
Serves 8.

Dinner at the Lake House
Fearless Recipes
page 75

Marinated Tomatoes with Shrimp

Mix together in a bowl:
1 C. fresh lemon juice
1 C. vegetable oil
1/2 C. fresh basil, minced
10-12 garlic cloves, pressed
1/2 t. garlic salt
1/2 t. salt
1/4 t. ground black pepper

Place in a shallow pan:
3 large tomatoes, sliced

Pour mixture over tomatoes, cover and refrigerate.

When ready to serve, set marinated tomatoes on a tray covered with a bed of lettuce.

2 lbs. shrimp, boiled and peeled
Feta cheese
Mozzarella cheese, sliced

Toss shrimp in balance of marinade and place with tomatoes.
Sprinkle with feta cheese.
Serve with sliced mozzarella.
Serves 6-8.

Mussel and Pepper Pasta

3-4 dozen mussels, cleaned and steamed as directed

Add to the water:
1/2 C. dry white wine
4 cloves of garlic, crushed

1 yellow bell pepper
1 orange bell pepper
1 red bell pepper
1 green bell pepper
1 large purple onion

Slice above in strips and lightly saute in:
 8 T. butter
 3 garlic cloves, crushed

In a microwave:
3 sticks of salted butter
7 garlic cloves, pressed
1/2 t. salt
8 oz. jar capers

Soften butter, add garlic and salt and microwave until melted.
Remove from microwave and add capers.

Angel Hair Pasta, cook as directed.

 Lightly toss pasta in butter/caper mixture.
Place in a large pasta bowl.
Add the sauted vegetables then the mussels, spooning balance of
butter/caper mixture over each mussel.

Sprinkle with feta or shredded parmesan cheese.
Serves 8.

Oyster and Artichoke Heart Stuffing

1 package of your favorite corn bread stuffing
1 pt. oysters, drained (cut smaller if needed)
1-2 C. marinated artichoke hearts, cut and drained
1/4 t. ground sage
Salt and pepper to taste

Prepare stuffing as directed, adding oysters, artichoke hearts and
seasonings, toss well.
Place in a casserole dish and bake at 350 degrees for approximately
20-25 minutes.

6 artichokes

Clean and cook artichokes as desired, making sure bottom is cut flat
in order for artichoke to sit up.
Remove center and fill cavity with stuffing. Slip stuffed artichokes
back in the oven in a baking dish for 10 minutes.
Garnish with a dab of butter and a sage leaf.
Serves 6.

Trout Amandine

3 lbs. trout fillets
1 1/2 C. milk
1 C. flour
Salt and pepper to taste
12 T. butter (2 sticks)
3/4 C. sliced almonds
4 T. lemon juice
2 T. parsley, chopped

Cover fillets with milk, refrigerate for 2-3 hours.
Drain, salt and pepper, then flour.
Saute in butter until golden brown.
Remove fish.
Add almonds, parsley and lemon juice to skillet.
Brown, stirring constantly.
Generously pour over fish.
Garnish with lemon slices and fresh parsley.
Serves 6.

Berry Cherry Cobbler

Crust

Whisk in a bowl:
 2 2/3 C. all-purpose flour
4 T. sugar
3 t. baking powder
1 t. salt

10 T. cold unsalted butter, cut into small pieces.
Cut butter into dry ingredients using two knives continuing in a
criss cross pattern until it resembles coarse bread crumbs.

Add:
2/3 C. heavy cream
2/3 C. sour cream
1 t. vanilla extract

Mix with a large wooden spoon until dough comes together
creating a ball.
Knead approximately 10 times.
Dust with flour, then pat and press out with your hands until 1/4"-
1/2" thick on a parchment-covered cookie sheet.
Brush dough with melted butter, and sprinkle with sugar.
Bake at 350 degrees for approximately 45 minutes.

Filling

1 can cherry pie filling
1 C. sugar
1 t. lemon zest
1/2 C. brown sugar
1/2 t. ground cinnamon

Heat in a sauce pan until all sugar dissolves. Remove from heat.

Add 1 C. fresh blackberries and toss.

Pour over broken biscuit dough.
Top with whip cream or vanilla ice cream, if desired.
Serves 6.

Pan Seared Tuna
with Stuffed Jalapeños and Avocado Cream

Stuffing

1 T. olive oil
2 T. yellow onion, finely chopped
2 t. garlic, minced

1 C. canned tomatoes, drained and chopped fine
2 t. sugar

1 T. parsley, chopped
2 T. raisins, chopped
2 T. Spanish olives, rinsed well and chopped
1 T. capers, rinsed well and chopped
1/8 t. dry oregano
1 t. salt

In a small saute pan, heat olive oil over medium flame. When hot, add in the onion and garlic and sauté until golden brown. Add in the tomatoes, reduce the heat and cook slowly until completely dry. The tomatoes should start to caramelize before continuing on.
Add the remaining ingredients and cook for 4-5 more minutes, stirring constantly. Adjust seasoning with salt.

Cool completely before stuffing peppers.

To prepare jalapenos peppers for stuffing:

12 large jalapenos
Using a paring knife, make a "T" cut in each jalapeno. To do this, slice across the top of the pepper just under the stem, being careful not to remove the top, and from the center of the first cut, slice the pepper lengthwise almost to the very tip. Gently pry the peppers open and remove the seeds and the white membrane. Wearing gloves is recommended during this process.

Fill two small pots with 1 quart of water. Add 1 C. sugar to one pot, and 2 T. salt to the other. Place them on a high flame and bring them to a boil.

Prepare an ice bath by filling a large bowl with lots of ice and water.

Drop the peppers in the boiling salted water first. Simmer for 30 seconds and using a slotted spoon, remove them from the boiling water and place them in the ice bath for one minute. Then place the peppers in the boiling sugar water. Simmer for 30 seconds. Again, remove them and place them in the ice bath. Repeat this process two more times so that the peppers are blanched three times in each pot.

Drain completely and fill each pepper with the stuffing. These may be made a day in advance.

Avocado Cream

1/2 of a fresh avocado
1 T. fresh lime juice
1/2 C. sour cream
1/2 t. salt
1/8 t. cayenne pepper
1 T. cilantro, finely chopped

Remove the avocado skin and smash the avocado and lime juice together to create a puree. Add in the remaining ingredients and beat until smooth.

Tuna

12 ounces fresh, sushi-grade tuna, cut into 2 ounce pieces, the thicker the better.
2 T. olive oil

Heat the olive oil in a sauté pan over high heat. Season the tuna with salt and fresh ground pepper. Once the oil is very hot, begin searing the tuna, this will require only 20-25 seconds of cooking time on each side of the tuna pieces. Make sure you are using a sauté pan large enough to hold all of the tuna with out overcrowding the pan, or sear the tuna in batches.
Once the tuna is seared, it is time to assemble the plates.
Place two stuffed jalapenos on each serving dish, cut the pieces of tuna in half, or slice them thinly (you'll need a real sharp knife to slice it thin without tearing it) and arrange the tuna with the jalapenos. Finish with a small dollop of the avocado cream on the side.

Pan Roasted Pork Chop with
Peach BBQ Sauce
Caramelized Onion and
Cheddar Cheese Grits

BBQ Sauce

1 T. bacon fat
1/4 C. yellow onion, diced
2 t. garlic, minced
1/2 t. fresh ginger, minced
2 t. fresh jalapeno, seeds removed and diced small
1/2 lb. fresh peaches, peeled, pit removed and sliced
2 t. tomato paste

1/2 C. brown sugar
1/2 C. ketchup
1/4 C. stock (veal or chicken)
1/4 C. orange juice

2 T. rice wine vinegar
1 t. soy sauce
1 t. Worcestershire sauce
1/2 cinnamon stick
1/8 t. each: ground coriander, cumin, chili powder
Pinch cayenne pepper
1 t. kosher salt
1/4 t. fresh ground black pepper
1 t. fresh thyme, chopped

In a 1 1/2 quart sauce pot, melt the bacon fat over a medium heat. Add in the onions and cook for 3-4 minutes. Add in the garlic, ginger, jalapenos, peaches and tomato paste and cook for 7-8 more minutes, stirring frequently to prevent the ingredients from sticking and burning.
Add in the remaining ingredients and bring the mixture to a very low simmer. Cook for 30-40 minutes, stirring frequently.
This sauce may be made up to five days in advance.

Caramelized Onion and Cheddar Cheese Grits

2 T. unsalted butter
1 1/2 C. yellow onion, thinly sliced
1 T. kosher salt
1 cup whole milk
1/3 cup chicken stock
1/3 cup grits
1 t. fresh ground pepper
3/4 C. extra sharp cheddar cheese, grated
In a 1 quart sauce pot, melt the butter over low-medium heat. Add the onions and salt, and cook until the onions are caramelized, about 10 minutes. Stir the onions often and be careful not to let them burn.
Add in the milk and stock and bring the liquid to a boil. Stir in the grits and lower the heat so that a low simmer is achieved. Stir constantly for 3-4 minutes, and then stir often for the next 12-14 minutes. Remove from heat and stir in the pepper and cheese. Allow grits to sit for 5-10 minutes before serving.

Pork Chops

6 double cut pork chops
2 T. olive oil
1-2 T. kosher salt
1 T. fresh ground black pepper

Preheat oven to 350 degrees.
Set a large 12" saute pan over a medium-high heat. Heat the oil in the sauté pan, and season all surfaces of each pork chop with the salt and pepper. Once the oil is hot, sear the surfaces of the pork chops until golden brown, about 5 minutes on each side.
Remove them from the saute pan, place them on a baking sheet, and place in oven.
Bake until the pork chops reach 150 degrees internal temperature, about 12-14 minutes.

Divide the grits between the serving plates. Place the pork chop resting up against the grits and place 2 ounces of warm BBQ sauce on each pork chop

Bittersweet Chocolate and Praline Tart

1 pie crust
1 recipe Pralines
12 ounces bittersweet chocolate, finely chopped
Vanilla ice cream

Pie Crust:

1 1/2 C. all purpose flour
1 T. sugar
1/4 t. salt
1 stick unsalted butter, cut into small pieces and chilled
1 T. vegetable shortening
1/4 C. ice water
1 T. lemon juice

Sift the flour, sugar and salt into a large bowl. Cut into butter and shortening, then using your fingers, rub the fats into the flour until the mixture resembles coarse crumbs.
Combine the water and lemon juice, and one tablespoon at a time, begin working the water mixture into the flour. Add just enough liquid until the dough comes together. Be careful not to over-mix.
Wrap the dough tightly in plastic wrap and refrigerate for at least 30 minutes. You may hold it refrigerated for two days.

Pralines

1 C. firmly packed brown sugar
1 C. granulated sugar
1/2 C. whipping cream
2 T. unsalted butter
2 t. vanilla extract
1/4 t. salt
1 C. chopped pecans

Place the sugars and cream in a heavy-duty sauce pot and bring to a boil over a medium heat, stirring constantly. When the mixture reaches 228 degrees, stir in the butter pieces, pecans, salt and vanilla, and continue to cook until the mixture reaches 236 degrees. Remove the pan from the heat and cool the mixture for 5 minutes. Stir the mixture with a wooden spoon for 3-5 minutes and pour it out onto a lightly oiled sheet pan. Cool completely. Then chop into medium-size pieces.

To Assemble Tart

Roll out the pastry on a lightly floured surface into a 12" circle, about 1/4" thick. Carefully roll the dough up onto the pin (this may take a little practice) and lay it inside a 9" tart pan with a removable bottom. Press the dough into the pan so it fits tightly; press the edges into the sides of the pan. It is important to press the dough evenly into every nook and corner of the ring, especially the scalloped edges. Shave off the excess hanging dough with a knife. Put the tart in the refrigerator for 15 minutes to relax.
Preheat the oven to 350 degrees.
Place the tart pan on a sturdy cookie sheet so it will be easy to move in and out of the oven. Line the tart with aluminum foil and add pie weights or dried beans to keep the sides of the tart from buckling.
Bake for 30 minutes, then remove the foil and weights. Using a pastry brush, lightly coat the crust with a beaten egg white. Return to the oven and continue to bake for another 12 minutes until the tart is golden brown in color.
Remove from the oven and evenly distribute half of the chopped chocolate onto the tart shell. Next fill the shell with the chopped praline pieces and then the remaining chocolate. Press the mixture down slightly, filling in the crevices with chocolate.
Return the tart shell to the oven for 5 minutes.
To cut the tart, gently press the bottom of the removable tart pan up through the top, and use a sharp serrated knife to cut wedges. Just before serving, place the tart in a 200 degree oven for 6-7 minutes. Place the tart pieces on the serving plates and top with vanilla ice cream.

Impromptu Picnic
Fearless Recipes
page 61

Henington House
Choco, Choco, Chocolate Chip Cookies

4½ C. flour
2 t. baking soda
1 t. salt

Combine ingredients. Set flour mixture aside

1½ C. sugar
1½ C. brown sugar
2 C. shortening (not butter)
2 t. vanilla
1 t. water
4 eggs

Beat until creamy.

Add flour mixture one cup at a time and mix well.

36 ounces bittersweet or semi sweet chocolate chips or chunks
(3 12-ounce bags)
2 C. chopped nuts (optional)

Stir into mixture.
Place dough on cookie sheet by the spoonful.
Bake at 325 degrees for 10 minutes.
Let cookies cool for a minute before removing.
Makes 10 dozen medium size cookies.

Iced White Grape Juice
and Ginger ale Punch

Mix:
1 part white grape juice
2 parts ginger ale

Serve over washed, frozen white grapes and ice.

"Cellar"bration
Recipes - Gourmet and More
page 66

Vegetable Confetti Squares

2 8-count crescent rolls, uncooked
3/4 C. mayonnaise
1/2 C. sour cream, softened
1 envelope ranch dressing mix
3 C. vegetables, finely chopped
(3/4 C. each: bell pepper, carrots, broccoli, green onions)
3/4 C. finely shredded cheddar cheese

Cover bottom of an 11x17 ungreased jelly roll pan (sheet cake pan)
with flattened crescent rolls. Make sure to press all seams together.
Bake at 375 degrees for 8-10 minutes or until lightly brown. Set
aside to cool. Mix together cream cheese, sour cream, mayonnaise
and ranch dressing.
Spread mixture over crescent rolls. Sprinkle vegetables over cream
cheese mixture. Pat down lightly. Sprinkle cheddar cheese over
vegetables. Cover with plastic wrap and chill for 3-4 hours. Cut into
squares and serve.
Makes 20 2x2 squares.

It's a Party! Marinated Shrimp

3 packages Seasons Italian dressing
2 large purple onions, sliced and ringed
2 14-oz. cans artichoke hearts, drained
2 jars capers
3 lbs. fresh, large shrimp, cooked and peeled

Prepare Italian dressing according to package instructions, omitting
the water and replacing with vinegar. Oil may be slightly reduced
if desired. Place shrimp, onions, artichoke hearts, mushrooms and
capers in a deep container. Add Italian dressing, making sure every
thing is well-coated. Marinate over night.
Serve on a bed of salmon if desired.
Serves 12.

Cheddar Bacon Dip

Mix together and spread in a 9" pie or quiche pan:
1 C. cheddar cheese, shredded
3 green onions, chopped
1/2 C. mayonnaise
8 oz. cream cheese, softened

Sprinkle over cheese mixture:
1 sleeve Ritz crackers, crushed.
10 strips of cooked bacon, crumbled.

Bake at 350 degrees for 20-30 minutes.

Serve with assorted breads or crackers.

Soup and Salad
Fearless Recipes
pages 87, 89 & 91

Corn and Crab Bisque

Saute until translucent:
1 stick salted butter
1 pkg. frozen white onions

Add:
3 cans crab meat, drained
2 cans creamed corn
1 C. heavy cream
1/2 t. fresh ground nutmeg

Mix well over heat.
Do not boil.
Sprinkle with nutmeg.
Serves 6.

Three Cheese Bread

Thaw frozen bread loaf and let rise in a greased bowl.
After bread has risen add 1/2 C. each of desired 3 cheeses, shredded or cut in chunks for "pops" of flavor.

We chose:
Sharp cheddar
Monterrey Jack
Parmesan

Knead cheeses into thawed, risen dough with 1/2 t. olive oil.
Then mound dough on a greased cookie sheet and let rise again.
Lightly spray or brush with olive oil or butter. Before baking, sprinkle parmesan cheese and bake as instructed.

Olive and Sun-Dried Tomato Bread

Follow three Cheese Bread recipe, replacing cheeses with olives and sun dried tomatoes. Marinated sun dried tomatoes can be used, just drain well and omit 1/2 t. oil.

Fiesta Stew

2 lb. ground sausage, cooked and drained
2 cans pinto beans, drained
2 cans kidney beans, drained
2 cans sweet corn, drained
2 cans diced tomatoes with liquid
1 8 oz. jar picante sauce
1 pkg. ranch dressing
1 pkg. fajita seasoning
1 pkg. taco seasoning

Dump all in a large Crockpot at medium heat, stirring occasionally.
Note: It will take quite awhile to heat this dish all the way through.
Serve with shredded cheese, sour cream, chopped green onions and tortilla chips.
Serves 12.

New England Clam Chowder

3 cans of your favorite clam chowder
Replace milk quantity with 1/2 heavy cream and 1/2 sour cream.
2 garlic cloves
1/2 t. rosemary
Add more clams if desired.
Heat as instructed. Thin with cream if needed.
Top with slice of butter and rosemary.
Serves 6-8.

Caesar Salad

Mix together:
1 bag romaine lettuce
1/3 C. parmesan cheese
1/2 large purple onion, sliced
Garlic onion croutons

Mix together for dressing.
1/2 C. Paul Newman's creamy caesar dressing
1/2 C. Girard's caesar dressing

Toss well right before serving.
Offer additional grated parmesan cheese on side.
Serves 6.

Carnival Cocktails
Fearless Recipes
page 104

New Orleans-Style Mini Muffulettas

Rolls in easy to pick up size
Olive salad (found in most grocery stores with olives)
Smoked ham, sliced
Genoa salami, sliced
Provolone cheese, sliced

Cut roll open width-wise (toast if desired).
Generously spread the olive salad on both sides.
Stack ham, salami and cheese.
Close sandwich and cut lengthwise.
Pile on a tray and serve.

Spinach Rolls

Prepared spinach spread or dip (found in most grocery stores)
Cloves of garlic, minced
Salt
Softened cream cheese (if needed for thickness)
Phyllo sheets
Salted butter, melted

If using a spinach dip you may need 4 oz. of softened cream cheese for thickness. It should be thin enough to spread well, not watery. Add garlic and salt for taste.

Butter both sides of phyllo sheets with a pastry brush, laying one on top of the other.
Spread spinach mixture on the top phyllo sheet leaving approximately 1/2" on each end. Roll the phyllo dough creating a long tube. Fold all ends in, using melted butter as paste to secure.

Lay on a cookie sheet covered with parchment paper.
Bake at 325 degrees for 18-20 minutes or until golden brown.
Let sit for 2-3 minutes. Cut at an angle and serve.

Shrimp Rolls

Prepared same as spinach rolls, substituting shrimp spread.

Anniversary Dinner
Recipes - Walnut Circle Grill
page 117

Veal Stuffed Mushrooms with Port Wine and Garlic Sauce

Veal Stuffing

1/2 pound ground veal
1 T. garlic oil
1 small clove garlic, chopped
1/2 C. chicken stock (broth)
1 C. Italian seasoned bread crumbs

Brown the veal in garlic oil. Reserve veal stock for sauce.
Add the garlic to the veal and sauté 3-5 minutes.
Add chicken stock and reduce liquid by half.
Add bread crumbs and sauté for an additional 3-5 minutes.
Remove from heat.

1/2 C. grated parmesan cheese

Mix parmesan into veal.
Season to taste with salt and pepper and allow mixture to cool.

20 large stuffing mushrooms, stems removed

Stuff each mushroom with 2 ounces of veal stuffing.
Place in baking dish.
Bake stuffed mushrooms at 350 degrees for 8 to 10 minutes. (until hot).
Add slices of mozzarella cheese to mushroom tops just prior to removing from oven.

Port Wine and Garlic Sauce

8 oz. veal stock, reduced
2 T. garlic, chopped
4 oz. port wine

Sauté garlic in saucepan. Add port and reduce by one half.
Add reduced veal stock.

Place mushrooms on plates and ladle sauce over mushrooms.
Serves 4.

Oven Roasted Rack of Lamb with Mint Demi-Glace Sauce

Blend in a processor:
5 garlic cloves
4 T. extra virgin olive oil
3 t. fresh rosemary, chopped
2 t. salt
1 t. ground black pepper

Make a paste and generously cover:
2 racks of lamb

Place on a baking sheet, cover and refrigerate for at least 3 hours.

Preheat oven 400 degrees.
Cook for 20 minute (medium-rare to medium).
Cut rack two ribs at a time.
Display and serve with Mint Demi-Glace.

Mint Demi-Glace
For ease we suggest buying a Demi-Glace Paste (most often found in gourmet shops) and follow as directed.
Add Creme De Mint to taste.
Drizzle over chops and serve.
Serves 4.

Walnut Circle Salad with Raspberry Vinaigrette

Dressing
1 C. walnuts
1 C. raspberry vinegar
1 pinch salt
1 pinch pepper
1 pinch herb de province
4 T. honey
2 T. roasted garlic

Blend all ingredients.

2 C. salad oil

Slowly pour salad oil into mixture until all ingredients are combined.
Blend dressing thoroughly.

Salad
1 package spring mix
1 carton cherry tomatoes
1 red onion, sliced
4 oz. goat cheese (Chevre), crumbled
1 C. roasted seasoned walnuts, coarsely chopped

Toss ingredients with dressing in large bowl.

Classic Creme Brulee

2 1/2 C. heavy whipping cream
1/2 t. vanilla extract
4 egg yolks
2/3 C. sugar

Put the cream over a pan of hot water. Heat slowly, do not boil.
Beat egg yolks with 5 T. of the sugar and vanilla. Stir in the cream.
Strain the custard and divide equally among 6 oven-safe containers.
Set in a roasting pan containing enough hot water to come halfway up the sides of the dishes. Bake in a preheated 300 degree oven until set, about 1 hour. Remove from the pan and let cool, chill for at least 4 hours.
Sprinkle remaining sugar over the top to form a layer and put under a hot broiler until the sugar melts and caramelizes, 2-3 minutes. Let cool 2-3 hours until the caramel layer is firm.
Serves 4-6.

Small Thanksgiving
Fearless Recipes
page 136

Rosemary and Orange
Cornish Game Hen

4 hens, clean as directed

Place in a generous sauce pan and heat:
Juice of 3 large oranges
1/4 cup chopped rosemary
1/2 cup brown sugar
2 cups salted butter

Once butter is melted, add:
4 washed oranges, cut into pieces small enough to stuff hen

Toss oranges in mixture, leave on medium to low heat until orange skin can be pierced, stirring as needed.
Remove from heat, spoon oranges into hen cavity.

Cook hens as directed, continuing to baste with balance of mixture.
Garnish with a slice of orange, pierced with a rosemary sprig.
Serves 4.

Olive and Caper Stuffing Tower

1 pkg. of your favorite corn bread stuffing
1/2 C. capers, drained (liquid set aside)
1/2 C. olives, chopped (liquid set aside)
Butter

Using your favorite packaged dressing, substitute half of the required water or broth with the liquid from olives and capers.
Double the amount of butter the recipe calls for. Prepare on stove as instructed, remove from heat and add capers and olives.

Make sure stuffing is moist enough to stay molded. If not, continue to add small amounts of liquid until it is. Spray generously the inside of individual molds with cooking spray. Press stuffing firmly into each mold. Place molds on a cookie sheet and heat in oven shortly before serving.
Stuffing should easily slip out of mold.
Drizzle with a hot mushroom gravy, if desired, and serve.
Serves 6.

Asparagus Wrapped with Bacon Pastry

12-16 asparagus spears, snap off ends
4-6 strips of bacon
3 crescent rolls uncooked, laid flat, cut in half lengthwise
Olive oil

Lightly cook bacon in the microwave. Remove and place on top of crescent roll strip.
Roll asparagus in olive oil, bunch 3-4 spears together and twist and wrap bacon/dough combination around each bunch. Anchor by pinching dough together if needed.
Place bunches on a cookie sheet.
Cook at 350 degrees until tender and pastry is golden brown.
Makes 4-6 bunches.

Thanksgiving Breakfast
Recipe - Longleaf Plantation
page 143

Fried Quail

8 quail, cleaned

In a large bowl mix:
1/2 gal. milk
1 T. meat tenderizer
1 T. Tony's seasoning

Drench quail in mixture and let sit for 3 hours.

In another large bowl mix:
2 C. self rising flour
1 T. salt
1 T. pepper
1 t. garlic powder

Preheat deep fryer to 325 degrees.
Drain quail.
Coat with flour mixture.
Deep fry until golden brown,
approximately 8 minutes.
Serves 8.

Bridal Brunch
Recipe - The Pastry Garden
page 175

Orange-Cranberry Muffins

1 1/4 C. dried cranberries
1/3 C. orange juice
2 C. all-purpose flour
2 t. baking powder
1/4 t. salt
1/2 C. unsalted butter
1 t. orange zest, grated
2/3 C. sugar
2 large eggs
1/2 C. milk
1 t. orange flavoring

Preheat oven to 400 degrees.
Spray muffin pan or use muffin papers in the tin.
In a sauce pan add cranberries and orange juice. Bring to a simmer, then turn off heat and let cool to room temperature. Drain off juice and set aside both juice and cranberries.
In large bowl, cream butter, orange zest, sugar, and flavoring until light and fluffy. Scrape sides. Add eggs one at a time, beating well after each addition. Add milk and remaining juice from cranberries.

In separate bowl sift together flour, salt, and baking powder.
Add flour mixture to butter mixture. Fold in until all incorporated.
        Do Not Over Mix!!
Place in tin and bake until golden brown.
Bake for 12 minutes.
Makes 1 dozen.

Crab Cakes with Remoulade Sauce

2 medium yellow onions, chopped
1 green bell pepper, chopped
1 red pepper, chopped
1/2 bunch green onions, chopped
1 t. garlic, minced
2 T. olive oil
Heat oil and saute the first five ingredients for 5 minutes.

Add:
1/2 t. black pepper
1/2 t. thyme
1 t. white pepper
1/4 t. cayenne pepper
1/2 t. onion powder
1/2 t. garlic powder
Continue cooking for 2-3 minutes.

Add:
4 oz. seafood stock.

Reduce by half.

Remove from heat and add:
2 1/2 C. bread crumbs
1 large egg, lightly beaten

Spread out on sheet pan to cool immediately.

Fold in:
1 lb. crab meat

Form into cakes about 1/2 inch thick.
Add 1/4 t. olive oil to heavy skillet.
Add cakes and fry in batches over medium heat for about 3-5 minutes per side, or until golden brown.
Makes 8 crab cakes.

Remoulade Sauce
Mix:
1 qt. mayonnaise
1 C. creole mustard
2 T. lemon juice
2 T. horseradish
1 t. seasoned salt
1/8 stalk of celery, minced
1/8 bunch of parsley, minced
1/4 medium onion, minced
1 t. garlic powder
Refrigerate.

Duck Salad with Apple Cinnamon Currant Sauce

Soak for one hour:
1 C. currants
1/4 C. brandy

Caramelize:
1/2 C. brown sugar
1/2 C. red wine vinegar

Add and reduce for one hour:
3 C. demi glace
1 C. apple cider
2 cinnamon sticks
1 C. apple, peeled and chopped

2 boneless duck breasts

Salt and pepper duck breasts.
Sear in a large pan, 3-4 minutes.
Place in a 400 degree oven for 6-7 minutes until medium rare.

Slice and fan duck on a bed of mixed greens
Top with:
Walnuts
Prosciutto
Goat cheese
Drizzle with Apple Cinnamon Currant Sauce
Serves 6.

Strawberry Custard French Toast

6 English muffins
8 oz. mascarpone cheese
8 oz. jar of strawberry preserves
Cut muffins in half and place bottom half in 13x9 baking dish.
Spread with mascarpone and top with preserves. Place the other half of muffin on top.

9 eggs
3/4 C. sugar
3 C. milk
In separate bowl, beat eggs and sugar. Mix in milk and pour into pan with English muffins.

Sprinkle cinnamon over dish and top each English muffin with a pat of butter. Bake at 375 degrees for 40 minutes.

Top with fresh sliced strawberries and sprinkle with powdered sugar to serve.
Serves 6.

Acknowledgments

It is hard to believe that by the time this book is released, close to two years will have passed. What began as only a dream and looked like a monumental task has come to fruition. As we spent late nights and long weekends working on this much-loved project we found ourselves reminded to practice our own advice. When things got wild we regrouped, took a deep breath, made sure our vision was realistic and took one step at a time. When things did not go as planned, we worked around, did without, or came up with something else to make it work. As the project got larger we surrounded ourselves with our families and friends who knew our strengths and weaknesses and, best of all, helped us laugh. In most cases we used what our clients already owned. And when the job got too big we called in the troops. We can now testify that we have put this sound advice to the test in every chapter and not once did it fail us.

That brings us to the real strength of this project: all these without whom this book would not exist. We begin with our families, whose patience, assistance, moral support and prayers were unwavering. Randall Strange lived and breathed this project right along with us, while many times picking up the slack on the home front. Brent Wallace, not only for his remarkable photography, but for his calm, kind spirit and his zeal for making everything beautiful. We thank the big "G" for his unbelievable vote of confidence and Author, Restaurateur, and Columnist Robert St. John, who, from the very beginning, shared with us his time, talents and vast knowledge on the art of writing, producing and promoting a book. Louis Young and Tishomingo Tree Press, (John David's "brother from another mother" as they often joked), spent hours and hours and somehow always got what we gave him to press and back. Amy Sproles Smith, who with her journalistic gifts, took over 240 pages of misspelled words and botched-up sentences and made sense of them without hassling us too badly. Our "lovely assistants" Nancy Lou Hansen, Julie Miller, Lucy Parkman, Aaryanne Preusch, Jillian Strange, Caroline Webb, Billie Jean Williams and Kathy Chase Young (dear family and friends) were always there with a smile on their face and a willingness to work no matter how crazy the task. We thank those who made the inclusion of food in this book possible: Mary and Sarah Halliwell with their expertise in the culinary arts and knowledge of wines; the members of The Original Home and Garden Club of Hattiesburg, and The Real Garden Club of Hattiesburg for contributing their no-nonsense recipes and serving as test kitchens; The Purple Parrot Cafe, 206 Front, Walnut Circle Grill, Gourmet and More, and The Pastry Garden, for sharing their establishments' recipes, menus and food preparation skills. Diane Elzey, Kym Garraway, Patsy Gray, Michelle Heidelberg, Pamela James, Jennifer Parsons, Robert Williams and Catherine's father, Reed Hansen, whose original art in the form of paintings, masks, calligraphy or wood carvings took the creative elements of this book to another level. We also thank all of the friends and clients who generously and graciously let us into their homes to dig in their cupboards and take hundreds of pictures (often only a few hours before greeting their guests), and to all of the businesses and professionals listed on the resource page whose examples of their specialties throughout this book illustrate that anything is possible in the world of entertaining.

We could not have done it without you. Thank you!

In the Midst of Disaster

Before August 29, 2005, disasters, when speaking of entertaining, might have addressed what to do if your soufflé fell or how to manage with ivory candles when you needed white. However, Hurricane Katrina changed all of that. Our area was not devastated like some, but we would be remiss if we did not mention what effect it had on this book. Yes, it pushed our schedule back, and some locations had to be rethought. But the direction it took us was quite different than what you might have imagined. We not only saw, but experienced, hospitality and warmth in its purest forms. This included people reaching out to each other, sharing or giving what little they had only minutes after the storm. Then, after making sure everyone was alright, the gathering began. Every night for a week, after working nonstop from sun-up to sun-down in the merciless Southern summer heat, with no electricity, and little water, everyone pulled together what food they had and headed to the next-door neighbor's house where a grill was intact. What might have been the most frustrating and fearful time in our lives turned into what may be the most memorable. Every night the gathering got larger; the laughter got louder; believe it or not, the food got better; and not surprisingly, the fashions got funnier. Those evenings are what got us through that tough time. We pray we never forget them, and the difference sharing a meal with others, along with laughter, can make.

It is truly a gift to entertain. No matter what the circumstances - do it fearlessly!

Locations

*The homes and events photographed in
"Fearless Entertaining" are those of
clients and friends of the authors.*

Resources

A- Gallery
Life Style Art Boutique
Gifts and Fine Art
601.584.6785

B' Ann's Drapery
Custom Drapery and Bedding
601.268.2230

Brent Wallace
Photography
601.794.6916

Classy Coverups
Fabric and Trim
228.896.9498

The Corner Market
Specialty Groceries
601.264.3425

Flathau's Fine Foods
Gourmet Cookies
601.582.9629

Forrest Paper Company
Custom Design, Invitations,
Stationery and Wrappings
601.545.7422

Tish Gammill
 Interior Design
The Home Collection
Interior Furnishings and Gifts
601.264.3326

Gourmet and More
Gourmet Gifts and Foods
Catering
601.261.9366

 The Kitchen Table
Sharing the Culinary Art
 of Entertaining
Fine Culinary Gifts
601.261.2224

Janice Mattern
Wedding Cakes
601.264.5129

McKenzie's on Main
Antiques and Gifts
601.544.2240

The Pastry Garden
Scratch Bakery and
 Wedding Cakes
601.271.2540

Perrier Party Rentals
Specialty Linens and
 Party Rental
504.834.8570

Photography by Erin
Erin Hicks
601.425.0004

Pink's
Paper and Presents
601.450.5252

Plum's
Decorative Accessories,
 Gifts and Bridal Registry
601.544.7586

Purple Parrot Cafe
Fine Dining
601.264.0656
Purple Parrot Caterers
601.264.0672

Tracey Robertson
The Bride's Bouquet
601.441.8089

Sanders Wholesale Florist
Sells to the Trade
601.544.4037

St. Martian's Gallery
Fine Antiques
601.362.1977

Showbiz Theatrical Lighting
 Services
251.473.2053

Taylor Rental
Party and Wedding Rental
601.261.5060

206 Front Restaurant
Fine Dining
601.545.5677

Tishomingo Tree Press
Digital Pre-press and Web Design
601.582.0116

Top it Off Rental Company
Specialty Linens and
 Party Rental
601.362.8861

Walnut Circle Grill
Fine Dining
Walnut Room Private Dining
601.544.2202

Walnut Square Old Town Gifts
Gifts and Ice Cream Parlor
601.543.0111

Copyright © 2006 John David Williams, Catherine Hansen Strange

Photography Copyright © 2006 Fearless Entertaining Press, LLC

First Edition, 2006 ISBN 0-9788366-1-8

Printed in The United States of America

Designed and Produced by John David Williams, Catherine Hansen Strange

Photography by Brent Wallace

Additional Photography by Erin Hicks: Pages 72 & 73; Pages 100 & 101, photo of sanctuary and candles; Page 110, photo of Chupphah; Pages 112 & 113

Electronic Pre-Press & Web Design by
Tishomingo Tree Press
606 Bay Street
Hattiesburg, Mississippi 39401
www.tishomingotree.com
info@tishomingotree.com

Fearless Entertaining Press, LLC
517 Rebecca Avenue No. 1
Hattiesburg, Mississippi 39401
www.fearlessentertaining.com
info@fearlessentertaining.com

PRESS